Prayers for Children

Compiled by Robbin Nicola

Illustrated by Pamela Key

*I'd like to dedicate this to my parents who kept me in church
and taught me to look for the good in everyday things.*

© 2006. Published by Journey Stone Creations, LLC.
All rights reserved. Printed in China. Little Gems is an imprint of
Journey Stone Creations, LLC. First print run, 2006.

ISBN# 1-59958-030-6

Please visit our web site for other great titles.
www.jscbooks.com

Thank You for the world so sweet,
Thank You for the food we eat,
Thank You for the birds that sing,
Thank You, God, for everything.
Amen

Now I lay me down to sleep,
I pray the Lord my soul to keep.
May Angels watch me through the night
And keep me in His blessed sight.
Amen

Thank you, God, both day and night,
For seeds and wheat and bread.
That all around this great wide world,
Your children will be fed.
Amen

Now the light has gone away,
Savior, listen while I pray,
Asking Thee to watch and keep
And to send me quiet sleep.
Amen

Forgive me if I have this day
Done any wrong in work or play.
Oh, help me always to do right,
And bless me every day and night.
Amen

Bless my Mom and my Dad,
Keep me safe from all things bad.
Watch over me all through the day,
Keep me safe while I play.
Protect me, Lord, throughout the night;
Help me wake with a smile so bright.
Amen

God bless Mom,
God bless Dad,
God bless every friend I have.
God bless Mamaw & Papaw too,
God bless everything I do.
Amen

Good morning, God,
Good morning, Day,
And Sun and Grass and Trees.
Good morning, Clock,
And all the hours
Of joy you bring to me.
I'm glad I am awake again;
I'm glad I can declare
Good morning, God,
I know You are
Right here, everywhere!
Amen

God, be my help in every need;
God, please, my every hunger feed;
God, walk beside me, guide my way
Through every moment of the day.
Amen

Guide and direct me,
Show me the way;
Help me, dear Father,
Through all this day.
Amen

Father, we thank Thee for the night
And for the pleasant morning light,
For rest and food and loving care
And all that makes this world so fair.
Help us to do the things we should,
To be to others kind and good;
In all we do, in all we say,
To serve Thee better, every day.
Amen

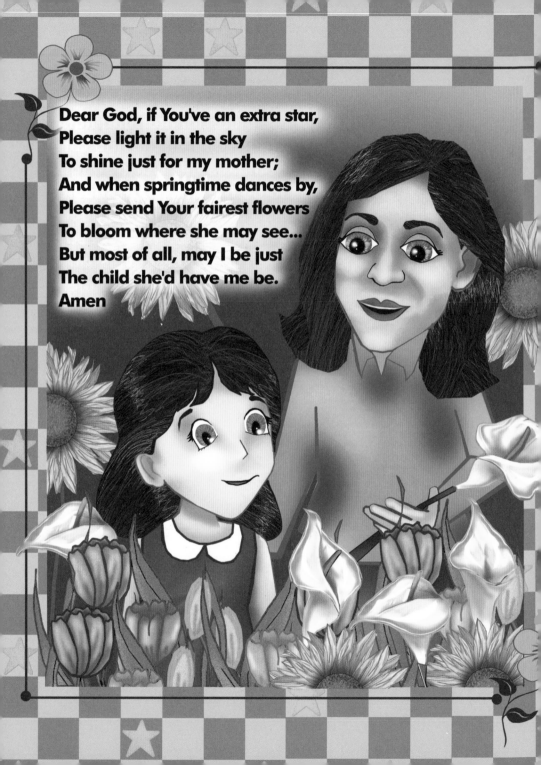

Dear God, if You've an extra star,
Please light it in the sky
To shine just for my mother;
And when springtime dances by,
Please send Your fairest flowers
To bloom where she may see...
But most of all, may I be just
The child she'd have me be.
Amen

Dear God, a hundred times a day,
Between my thanks for other things,
A special little thank you song
My heart with gladness sings.
A special little song of thanks
Because, dear God, You see,
Of all the Dads on earth, I'd choose
The one You gave to me!
Thank you for everything.
Amen

Dear God, with Thy help I know
This year tall and strong I'll grow.
I'll be good at home and school
And always keep the golden rule.
Keep me safe from all harm's way,
Protect me, Lord, this I pray.
Amen

I thank You, Lord, for all the good
That comes each happy day:
For pleasant homes and gentle friends,
For restful sleep and play.
I thank You for the birds and trees
That make the summer fair,
For shining stars and rippling streams,
For winter's tingling air.
Amen

A simple meal can be a feast;
Where there's love, the food's the least!
Mother says just bread and tea
Is a feast when all agree
And speak kindly to each other
And thank You for one another.
Thank You, God.
Amen

Guide and direct me,
Show me the way;
Help me, dear Father,
Throughout each day.
Amen

It is very nice to think
Our world is full of meat and drink,
For little children saying grace
In every Christian kind of place.
Thank You, God, for everything.
Amen

I love to hear the autumn wind
And smell the buds of May.
I loved the starry sky last night,
My glass of milk today.
And so I'd like to say, dear God,
Wherever You may be,
That oftentimes I stop and think
How good You are to me.
Amen

Good night, dear God, another day has ended;
Again to us Thy night sweet slumber brings.
Again Thy children sleep; again we pray
Thee to keep us in the shadow of Thy wings,
Another day.
Amen

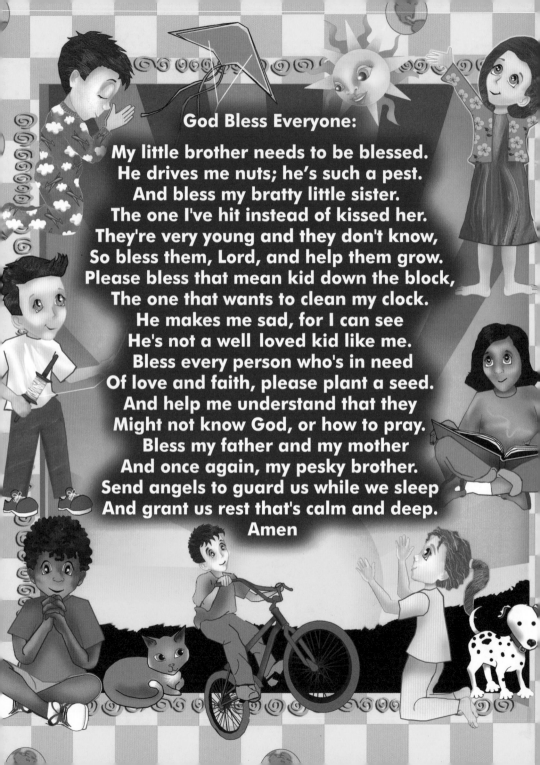

God Bless Everyone:

My little brother needs to be blessed.
He drives me nuts; he's such a pest.
And bless my bratty little sister.
The one I've hit instead of kissed her.
They're very young and they don't know,
So bless them, Lord, and help them grow.
Please bless that mean kid down the block,
The one that wants to clean my clock.
He makes me sad, for I can see
He's not a well loved kid like me.
Bless every person who's in need
Of love and faith, please plant a seed.
And help me understand that they
Might not know God, or how to pray.
Bless my father and my mother
And once again, my pesky brother.
Send angels to guard us while we sleep
And grant us rest that's calm and deep.
Amen